SELF-DEFENSE FOR RADICALS
BY MICKEY Z.
PMPRESS

PM Press PAMPHLET SERIES

PM Press PAMPHLET SERIES No. 0008
SELF-DEFENSE FOR RADICALS: A TO Z GUIDE FOR SUBVERSIVE STRUGGLE
By Mickey Z.
ISBN: 978-1-60486-204-1

PM Press
PO Box 23912
Oakland, CA 94623
www.pmpress.org

Layout and design: Daniel Meltzer

Printed in Oakland, CA on recycled paper with soy ink.

"RADICAL SIMPLY MEANS GRASPING THINGS AT THE ROOT."

—ANGELA DAVIS

"WE ARE NONVIOLENT WITH PEOPLE WHO ARE NONVIOLENT WITH US."

—MALCOLM X

"SOMETIMES I THINK THE WORLD IS DIVIDED INTO THOSE WHO HAVE A COMFORTABLE RELATIONSHIP WITH POWER AND THOSE WHO HAVE A NATURALLY ADVERSARIAL RELATIONSHIP WITH POWER."

—ARUNDHATI ROY

"THE QUICKEST WAY TO A MAN'S HEART IS THROUGH HIS CHEST."

—ROSEANNE BARR

ACKNOWLEDGMENTS

My deep appreciation to Craig O'Hara and everyone at PM Press

Much gratitude to Rick for his cartoons

http://www.theplebsite.com

Thanks to pattrice for her input and help

Special thanks to Nancy Ryan and Mark Hand for friendship and support

Thank you, as always, to my wife and partner Michele, to my ever-supportive Dad, and to the enduring memory and influence of my beloved Mom

In memory of James Langergaard

TABLE OF CONTENTS

LET'S IMAGINE . . .

Let's imagine you step outside to get some air and see one of your friends lying on the ground. Standing above her is a large, menacing man with bad intentions and clearly, he has incapacitated your friend with a surprise blow. Her eyes meet yours and indicate she needs help.

WHAT WILL YOU DO?

You could pray. You could meditate. You could chalk it up to bad karma. You could ask your friend to recognize that the attacker is a human and tell him that she loves him. You could blame patriarchy, the Republicans, or gangsta rap. You could ask yourself: What would Jesus do? What would the Dalai Lama do? What would Oprah do? You could try to remember that excellent saying about non-violence you got from your Pilates teacher.

OR:

You could stomp your foot to draw his attention downward and promptly whip out a finger jab to his eyes. When he brings his hands up (too late) to protect himself, he leaves his midsection exposed. You kick him in the balls—doubling him over—then grab him by the hair and bring his face down into a powerful knee blow. Then you grab your friend and get the fuck out of there as fast as you can.

It's either *that* or chanting. The choice is yours.

Learning how to fight and/or defend yourself is not the same as promoting belligerent, anti-social behavior. We live in an exceedingly violent society. Our films, books, TV shows, and video games glorify mayhem and carnage. Our leaders (*sic*) solve most of their problems through aggression...or the threat thereof. While talk of non-violence is understandable and the struggle for peace has never been more essential, let's face it: the odds are, that sooner or later you're going to end up in a confrontation that may escalate into physical violence. So, why not be prepared?

AWARENESS

Don't worry…I'm not talking about *that* kind of awareness (see below). Instead, our opening letter refers to how we navigate the terrains we encounter. If someone is planning to attack you, odds are that the plan hinges on taking you by surprise. Thus, if the first line of self-defense is prevention, your safety just may depend on how aware you appear to be. Not paranoid, not afraid…but rather, a levelheaded state of alertness.

SUGGESTIONS:

- When walking or jogging alone, don't wear an iPod
- Vary your normal routes and routines
- When asked for directions by a driver, maintain a safe distance from the car
- Don't allow your gas tank to get too low. Running out of gas in an unfamiliar area is an unsafe situation.
- Avoid poorly lit areas
- See W for possible weapons
- If a car circles or passes you twice, let the driver know that you've noticed. Make eye contact and perhaps pull out your phone. The same goes for anyone who makes you nervous—driving or walking.

ON ANOTHER NOTE: Everywhere I hear about the need to raise that other kind of "awareness." So much so, that awareness and consciousness appear to have become ends in and of themselves. If only we were conscious of "what's going in Darfur" or aware of how "prevalent cancer has become" or whatever else we need to recognize, it seems most folks would be mighty satisfied.

My question: When exactly does all this goddamned awareness translate into productive action and tangible change?

We're aware of global warming and its causes, factory farms, war crimes, environmental degradation, political corruption, fixed elections, the health care crisis…blah, blah, blah. We know about it. We talk about it. We write about it. We complain about it. We hold meetings, talks, seminars, and classes about it. We march about it. We make signs about it. Nothing changes.

LESSON #1: Awareness is overrated

LESSON #2: The current patterns of dissent in America are long overdue for re-evaluation and overhaul. The powers-that-be have long ago figured out how to either marginalize or co-opt dissent. Until our tactics evolve, we remain accomplices to the perpetual global crime we call *civilization*.

Bite

You don't have to be Mike Tyson or Bela Lugosi to appreciate the might of the molars. A well-timed and well-placed bite can take a chunk out of any attacker's confidence. Anyone who chooses to assault you is fair game for a flesh breaking bite… so open wide and dish out the pain.

If this sounds too harsh, consider the obvious: the life you save may be your own.

Cheat

The ideal scenario, of course, would be to stop a fight before it occurs. This could happen if you developed (or faked) a rep and thus intimidated your opponent(s); if you talked your way out of the situation; or if you simply ran like hell. But, if none of these reasonable options work, it makes a whole lot of sense to land the first shot.

Back in my juvenile delinquent days, there was a guy we called Ratt who earned hero status as a fighter thanks to one straightforward tactic—landing the first shot. At the first whiff of trouble, Ratt would snap out a hard right hand and I never saw anyone recover sufficiently to win the fight. This is not to say you start tossing haymakers every which way but loose, but there's a glorious logic to taking the offensive when all other options are denied. Plus, you send a powerful message to your opponent(s) when you demonstrate that you're willing to take things to the next level.

Some may derogatively call this method a "sucker punch" or "fighting dirty" but when you're in a scrap, there are no rules. The best street fighters I've known have understood this reality. I'm thinking specifically about a guy named Steve, a massive football player with freakish strength who taught me some great pugilistic tricks. I remember watching him play handball with some guys from another neighborhood. An argument ensued and one of the strangers foolishly called Steve out. His next move was even more imprudent. The guy, who had a good physique and wanted to show it off, started to remove his shirt. Steve waited until the shirt was covering the guy's face before launching a sledgehammer right hand. The fight was over in a matter of seconds.

Ironically, I used an analogous ploy on Steve's younger brother, Paulie. Everyone thought he could take me so we ended up having a somewhat "play" fight in the schoolyard. I was holding my sneakers at the time (gym class was looming). As Paulie neared me with mayhem in his eyes, I tossed the sneakers at his face. When he ducked and covered his face, I pounced on him and got him in a headlock. The nuns broke it up but Paulie never bugged me again after that.

Another option (in case your running shoes aren't handy) is to keep plenty of change in your pocket. This way, if cornered into a fight you did not seek, you can reach into your pocket, grab the coins, and give 'em a hard toss at your enemy's groin. Like clockwork, he'll lower his guard to protect his sensitive parts, leaving his cocky mug wide open for a devastating opening salvo.

Of course, there are plenty of "dirty" tactics to employ when landing that all-important first shot, e.g. foot stomp, finger jab to the eyes, and the old reliable groin kick (as Bruce Lee sez: "I fear not the man who has practiced 10,000 kicks once, but I fear the man who has practiced one kick 10,000 times").

DALTON'S RULES

In the 1989 film *Roadhouse*, Patrick Swayze plays James Dalton, head bouncer at the seedy Double Deuce Club. Dalton is armed with a PhD in philosophy from New York University and three rules:

1. Never underestimate your opponent
2. Take it outside
3. Be nice until it's time to not be nice

NOTE TO THOSE STRIVING FOR JUSTICE AND ENDURING SOCIAL CHANGE:

It's time to not be nice.

ELBOWS

There's a reason why elbow strikes are against the rules in professional boxing. Even for such a brutal sport, this pointy weapon is considered too dangerous.

Aim those elbows at eyes, temple, throat, jaw, and groin. Be sure to get your hips and waist into it to add some power to the strike. And why stop at one? If your elbow lands cleanly, follow it up with a few more strikes if the opening remains.

THE F WORD

What is feminism? My favorite definition comes from the inimitable bell hooks: "A movement to end sexism, sexual exploitation, and oppression." This description not only exposes any non-feminist as the dogmatist he/she is, it also dovetails nicely with the concept of self-defense.

First, there are the three iniquities feminism seeks to abolish (sexism, sexual exploitation, oppression). So many physical attacks are essentially oppressive gestures spawned by a perceived ability to exploit a weaker (sic) gender. Therefore, any struggle to eradicate such gestures is by definition self-defense. Whether the person fighting back is female or male is not the point. However, the vastly greater number of female targets (see "S" for "Statistics") consequently creates more female fighters.

Second, bell hooks uses the word "movement." In a literal sense, self-defense requires movement: evading attack and then getting away from the scene as quickly as possible (see "R" for "Run").

FIGHTING BACK IS FEMINISM IN ACTION.

GOUGE

The vulnerability of a body part often depends on the attacker's physical make-up. For example, if a man has thick legs, he may not be the best candidate for a groin kick—a strike that requires a certain amount of precision.

However, the eyes are almost always available as a target. Even glasses usually can't prevent the attacker from reflexively raising his hands to his face. A man can be large. He can be a trained fighter. He can be in peak physical condition. He can be mentally unstable. Regardless of any of this, his eyes remain vulnerable.

Like "B" for "Bite," this entry is a tad stomach churning but remember: you didn't ask to be attacked. Therefore, you are free to do whatever it takes to defend yourself. To eschew this powerful weapon is to drastically reduce your chances of survival.

HEAD BUTT

Here's where being thick-headed pays off. So many attacks begin with a man grabbing you from behind. With his arms wrapped around you, he cannot protect his eyes, nose, and mouth. Nod your head forward, then drive it backwards forcefully into his exposed and vulnerable face. Then do it again.

**AND THEN ONE MORE TIME . . .
JUST TO MAKE SURE.**

INDIVIDUALITY

"When there is freedom from mechanical conditioning, there is simplicity. The classical man is just a bundle of routine, ideas, and tradition. If you follow the classical pattern, you are understanding the routine, the tradition, the shadow—you are not understanding yourself."

—BRUCE LEE

There is purity in the street fighter. He or she reacts without the "benefit" of organized training. Every punch, every duck, every kick, every block, every action—for better or for worse—is an expression of self, uncluttered by memorized forms and moves. This is precisely why many seasoned martial artists stand no chance against a confident bar brawler. A self-aware fighting stance is much more true to life than the lessons our teachers attempt to pass on.

> **BRUCE LEE SEZ**: *"All fixed set patterns are incapable of adaptability or pliability. The truth is outside of all fixed patterns."*

Enroll that same street fighter at your local karate school and you will witness a dramatic change. Too much time and effort is now dedicated to remembering what one is "supposed to do" instead of just "doing." What was once automatic becomes robotic. Ask a room full of fifty humans to write a story about love and you will get fifty unique tales. Walk into a typical karate school and you will watch fifty students being taught identical techniques. No two people write (or draw or sing) the exact same way, why should any two people fight the exact same way?

Toss an object at someone and they will instinctively block it or duck. No energy is wasted figuring out the right tactic to employ. It must be this way...for how can we expect to defeat a fearsome, ruthless enemy if we are unable to adapt to changing, fluid situations?

> **BRUCE LEE SEZ**: *"Always be yourself, express yourself, have faith in yourself, do not go out and look for a successful personality and duplicate it."*

Fighting skill comes full circle when someone who is able to maintain the beginner's mind of a street fighter combines that freedom with the conditioning and skills learned in a more formal setting. Zen writer Suzuki sez: "In the beginner's mind, there are many possibilities, but in the expert's mind there are few." The enlightened fighter who instills fear and respect in the heart of his or her opponent is the fighter not troubled by labels, titles, credits, or rankings. The primary concern is results.

To emerge victorious when facing down the challenges our violent society will inevitably present, we must heed these words of Bruce Lee:

"MAN, THE LIVING CREATURE, THE CREATING INDIVIDUAL, IS ALWAYS MORE IMPORTANT THAN ANY ESTABLISHED STYLE OR SYSTEM."

JUSTICE

For a while, I worked the night shift in a midtown Manhattan corporate gym (cue the shame and self-loathing). One night, I was wearing a Yankees t-shirt with the name "Justice" emblazoned on the back, for former Yank David Justice. An older woman (read: maybe in her late sixties) named Mary asked me if I was a Yankee fan. I told her yes, I was...but that my real reason for wearing the shirt was all about the word "justice." She smiled and declared that justice was a "noble idea." I braced myself for the inevitable "we need to show those towel heads some justice," but instead, this woman told me—albeit in a whisper—she was going to Washington to march against the war.

After this confession, Mary looked genuinely nervous. Had she gone too far? I leaned closer and said: "Don't worry, I'm with you."

Mary and I proceeded to talk each time she came to workout. The company eventually phased out the gym but just before my last day, I saw Mary and complimented her on how hard she was training.

She leaned close to me and whispered:

"WHEN THE REVOLUTION COMES, I'LL BE READY."

Knees & Knuckles

The elbow (see "E") isn't the only pointy bone in your toolbox (see "T"). A fist gives you four sharp knuckles and most of us have two knees. That makes two elbows, eight knuckles, and two knees: ten weapons to be used without hesitation or remorse.

Left Hook

"A great left hook consists of a bunch of precise separate movements that come together and appear as one smooth movement."
—JOE GOOSEN, PRO BOXING TRAINER

POWER FROM THE LEFT:

I first learned the power of the left hook at City Star Kickboxing Gym. I trained there—well before cable TV turned kickboxing into a spectacle—with some contenders and some champions. I also helped Enrique, the owner and head trainer, put out a pretty good kickboxing newsletter for a while...but like everyone else, I had to prove myself in the ring.

Early on, I got matched to spar with a guy named Phil. He was well liked, a little bigger than me, but I didn't think much of him as a fighter. Insulted to be regarded in his class, I circled Phil deftly and waited for him to make a move. Once he committed, I evaded the strike and took advantage of the subsequent opening...putting him down with a short, sharp left hook that bloodied his nose. I took a second to gaze at my gloved left hand in wonder while everyone in the gym went nuts and Phil struggled to his feet. They stopped it right there. A good moment...in that macho, twenty-year-old sort of way.

> **BRUCE LEE SEZ**: *"A smaller man who can swing faster may hit as hard or as far as the heavier man who swings slowly."*

Contrary to popular opinion, cinematic fisticuffs, and fighters with poor fundamentals, the hook is not a wide, looping punch that originates somewhere in left field and leaves the puncher exposed. They call it a "hook" precisely because your arm position should resemble a hook: a 90-degree angle at the elbow with your palm facing down at the point of impact.

SOME BASICS:

- Tuck your chin down into your left shoulder.
- Pivot your hips, waist, and front left foot in the direction of the punch: torque your whole left side. This will generate power without expending too much energy or movement.
- The hook can be thrown as part of a combination (e.g. jab-cross-hook or jab-hook) or as a single punch to catch an attacker.
- Mix up your targets: hook to the head, the body, or double up.

When using a left hand leading stance, your left hook is essentially thrown outside of your opponent's vision. (Using a right hook in such a stance can leave you wide-open for a counter.) The hook is an economical blow that, when executed properly, brings the full force of your body weight with it and is awfully tough to see coming. A knockout blow, it can stop a charging opponent in his or her tracks and change the momentum of any battle.

Postscript: City Star Kickboxing Gym eventually closed because Enrique went off to fight in El Salvador (I'm not sure for which side).

MOTHER LOVE

When I was about four or five years old, I came down with a mysterious ailment that involved debilitating leg pain, the inability to walk, and an irregular heartbeat. For a while, my pediatrician thought I might have rheumatic fever. My ever-devout mother prayed nightly for God to spare me and give her the condition.

Here's the catch: I soon recovered fully and my Mom came down with rheumatic fever, severe rheumatoid arthritis, heart problems, and more. These issues hampered her health for the rest of her life.

I'm not big on god, prayer, and all that. However, there's one thing of which I am 1000 percent certain: my mother meant it with all her heart when she said she'd rather suffer her entire life than see me sick. That's all the divine intervention I ever needed and that's the kind of Mother Love I'm talking about.

AND, AS DERRICK JENSEN REMINDS US:

Love does not imply pacifism.

No...

...means no.

OUTSIDE (THE LAW)

EMMA GOLDMAN SEZ: *"No great idea in its beginning can ever be within the law. How can it be within the law? The law is stationary. The law is fixed. The law is a chariot wheel which binds us all regardless of conditions or place or time."*

PROTECT YOURSELF

HANDS UP

Muhammad Ali screwed up the generation of fighters that followed him. Hands dangling at his sides, The Greatest dared his opponents to hit him. In the years before he was shamefully stripped of his title, the freakishly talented Ali could get away with breaking basic rules in such a blatant manner. Unfortunately, few have learned from witnessing the post-comeback punches Ali endured and, as a result, warriors are everywhere leaving their faces exposed...without enough vision and speed to pull it off.

A shitload of bad martial arts flicks have added another component: dropping one's hands when executing a kick. Unlike the lucky celluloid combatants we foolishly try to emulate, such a glaring error leaves a street fighter wide open for a counter. But fear not, remedying this situation is just a matter of conditioning. For this, I suggest you throw in the towel:

Wrap a small towel around the back of your neck and loosely grip the ends with both hands in front of you at chest height and your elbows in—a position that somewhat simulates a fighting on-guard stance. Position yourself in front of a mirror and start kicking. At first, you'll feel your balance thrown off and your elbows will be flapping like a goddamn chicken. But, like with all new motor patterns, you'll adjust over time. Gripping the towel will slowly build up a natural reflex to keep your hands up, protecting your head and upper body while launching your attack.

CHIN DOWN

Have you ever felt the jarring effects of a solid connection to your jaw? If so, you'll agree that even once is too much. The cause of such a debilitating blow just may be the fact that you carry your chin too high. Especially during in-fighting, a fighter should never leave his or her chin up as a target.

To aid in developing the habit of properly tucking one's chin, try taking one of your bag gloves or a knee pad or anything else that is soft and of similar size and placing it under your chin by pinning it up against your upper chest and neck. With the object tightly held in place, try some drills: speed bag, timing ball, shadowboxing, heavy bag, or even light sparring. The idea, of course, is to not allow the object to fall out during training.

Eventually, such practice will develop a reflex-like reaction to naturally keep your chin out of harm's way and you'll be a much better fighter for it. A tucked-in chin takes away one major target from your opponent(s). With those hands up and that chin down, you're no longer an easy victim; you become a more daunting challenge, and you put yourself in position to dictate the terms of the struggle.

QUICK ON YOUR FEET

"The battlefield is a scene of constant chaos. The winner will be the one who controls that chaos, both his own and the enemy's."
—NAPOLEON BONAPARTE

What if you've been preparing and you've cultivated speed, power, endurance, and accuracy—but can't get from point A to point B? Fast kicks and powerful punches can be rendered useless if you can't bridge the gap between yourself and your opponent(s). Footwork is what gets you there (and back). The ability to "explode" from your on-guard stance just may the most important physical skill you can learn as a fighter.

In conjunction with effective footwork comes the ability to strike while in motion. Once you've gotten from point A to point B, you must be able to exploit that accomplishment by landing a blow and getting out before you are hit with a counter. While punching in motion is certainly easier than kicking in motion, both require intense practice and study. The first step to effective footwork is analyzing your on-guard stance.

BRUCE LEE SEZ: *"Do not be tense, just be ready, not thinking but not dreaming, not being set but being flexible. It is being 'wholly' and quietly alive, aware and alert, ready for whatever may come.*

MISTAKES TO AVOID

- **Too much weight on either foot:** you must distribute your weight evenly or else your mobility will be severely hampered.
- **Improper distance between your feet:** if your stance is too wide, mobility becomes difficult and it is nearly impossible to strike without telegraphing your intent. If you are too close, all spring action is eliminated.
- **Stance too square:** standing in a straight-on position can make you an easy mark for a leg sweep and will not allow for quick backwards movements.

- **Improper hand position:** If your hands are too high, the lower torso is exposed. Too low and the face becomes an easier target. Keeping your hands too close to your body can invite your opponent to violate your space without any opposition from you. Conversely, if you overextend your arms, you limit your striking power.

SOME TIPS

- Your lead shoulder should be slightly raised to meet your chin (which should be slightly lowered).
- Use your forearms and elbows to protect your mid-section.
- Knees are bent at a subtle angle with your heels ever-so-slightly raised to assume a "coiled" position, ready to strike.

BRUCE LEE SEZ: *"Like the cobra, your strike should be felt before it is seen."*

Once your stance has been honed and refined to your own needs, the crucial concept of footwork can begin to take shape. Polished footwork skills (growing out of a secure on-guard stance) will enable you to move quickly in any direction and, most importantly, to hit without getting hit yourself.

NAPOLEON BONAPARTE SEZ: *"If you start to take Vienna, take Vienna."*

To make such a quick and successful advance on your opponent, it is first necessary to make a commitment. Thus, you must attack wholeheartedly or you will become vulnerable to a counterattack. To propel yourself forward "wholeheartedly" involves the shuffling of your feet followed by an explosive push-off. Clearly, this is not a simple case of hurtling oneself in the general direction of one's opponent. Rather, you are simultaneously gauging distance, monitoring patterns, and discerning openings until the time is right to bridge the gap explosively and without reservation.

MICKEY Z. SEZ: *"The shortest distance between this point and that point is simplicity."*

RUN

There is no shame in running. Some guy named Sun Tzu once said: "It is best to win without fighting." Keep yourself in running shape and—whenever possible—seek a safe path to escape from danger. If you are forced to engage, and able to deliver a debilitating blow, do so and then run away.

Statistics

- A woman is raped every 46 seconds in America (that's 78 rapes per hour)
- Every day, four women are killed by abusive partners
- 25 percent of girls and 17 percent of boys will be sexually assaulted by the time they are eighteen years old
- 14 percent of all American women acknowledge having been violently abused by a husband or boyfriend
- 28 percent of all homicides of women are domestic violence related
- 95 percent of reported domestic assaults involve victims who are female and perpetrators who are male
- 75 percent of rapes are committed by men the victims know
- In 2005, 1,181 women were murdered by an intimate partner. That's an average of three women every day.
- According to the National Center for Injury Prevention and Control, women experience about 4.8 million intimate partner-related physical assaults and rapes every year
- 17.6 percent of women in the United States have survived a completed or attempted rape. Of these, 21.6 percent were younger than age twelve when they were first raped, and 32.4 percent were between the ages of twelve and seventeen
- According to the National Crime Victimization Survey, which includes crimes that were not reported to the police, 232,960 women in the U.S. were raped or sexually assaulted in 2006. That's more than 600 women every day.
- Somewhere in America a woman is battered, usually by her intimate partner, every 15 seconds.

In 2007, 1,460 hate crime offenses based on sexual-orientation bias were reported by law enforcement agencies. Of these offenses:

- 59.2 percent were classified as anti-male homosexual bias.
- 24.8 percent were reported as anti-homosexual bias.
- 12.6 percent were prompted by an anti-female homosexual bias.
- 1.8 percent were the result of an anti-heterosexual bias.
- 1.6 percent were classified as anti-bisexual bias.

According to the Bureau of Justice, during the three years from 2003 to 2005, 47 States and the District of Columbia reported 2,002 arrest-related deaths by police.

TOOLBOX

ANI DIFRANCO SEZ: *"Every tool is a weapon if you hold it right."*

Let's say you're a handy man/woman/person and you get hired for a job. I'm guessing you'd bring your full toolbox to the worksite. After all, you can never be sure what might pop up and what tools you'll need. In other words, if you have a job to do, it would be illogical to decide beforehand that certain tools are off limits. Keep all your tools at your disposal—even if some remain permanently untouched—just in case.

Similarly, let's say you find yourself in a fight with a dangerous opponent. Would you rather have a hand grenade or a knife? Before you jump at the chance to blow someone up, contemplate the possibility that this fight could be happening in an elevator or on a crowded dance floor. Again, the situation dictates the tactics. It pays to be prepared and open-minded.

Case in point: *High Noon*. For me, the most powerful moment in the film is when Amy (Grace Kelly), the converted Quaker wife of Marshal Kane (Gary Cooper), shoots and kills a man to save her husband's life.

Earlier in the film, Amy declares: "My father and my brother were killed by guns. They were on the right side but that didn't help them any when the shooting started. My brother was nineteen. I watched him die. That's when I became a Quaker. I don't care who's right or who's wrong. There's got to be some better way for people to live."

However, Amy not only ends up shooting a man, she fights off the main villain, which allows Marshal Kane to finish him off.

High Noon was originally created as a McCarthy-era allegory. Today it stands as a stark warning not only that the average citizen would rather pretend all is well than stand up and fight but also that: *when staring down murderous psychopaths, even pacifists must sometimes choose to use an unexpected tool.*

UNITY

Try not to travel alone.
Don't stand by and let others be attacked.
Organize local groups and classes to spread the word.
In unity and collective action, there is strength.

VOICE

Scream for help.
Scream at your attacker as you fight back and kick his ass.
Scream into his ear and burst his goddamned eardrums.
Speak out against violence and the culture that encourages it.
Never remain silent in the face of injustice.

ONE EXCEPTION:
When dealing with the police, remember these magic words:
I am going to remain silent. I would like to see a lawyer.

WEAPONS

TO NAME BUT A FEW:

- Keys
- Umbrella
- Belt
- Pen
- Comb
- Fork
- Cell phone
- Books
- Bottles
- Cups
- Cane
- Broom
- Mop
- Shovel
- Flashlight
- Cords
- Towel
- Scarf
- Hot drinks
- Pocket change
- Imagination

IT'S BEEN SAID: *You are the weapon. Everything else is a tool.*

X FACTOR

There are more than individual attackers threatening us…for example:

- Number of synthetic chemical products found in the average American home: 63
- Pounds of chemicals used each year by the institutional cleaning industry: 5 billion
- 33 percent of personal care products contain at least one chemical linked to cancer
- 13 million tons of toxic chemicals are released around the world every 24 hours
- 70,000 people nationwide die prematurely each year from heart and lung disease aggravated by particulate air pollution
- 81 tons of mercury are emitted into the atmosphere each year by electric power generation
- According to the EPA, power plant emissions cause 2,800 lung cancer deaths each year
- More than 100 active pesticide ingredients are suspected of causing cancer, birth defects, and gene mutation
- 2.2 billion pounds of pesticides are used by Americans each year
- The risk of death from heart attack for the average American is 50 percent
- The risk of death from heart attack for a vegan: 4 percent

YOU GET THE IDEA…

Defend yourself against our poisonous culture.

(For starters, embrace not the corporate sanctioned standard American diet; go vegan, organic, and local.)

YARBLES

YARBLES, TESTICLES, COJONES, ONIONS, BALLS...

"Balls" is a male-centric term. Metaphorically speaking anyone can display "balls" by refusing to submit. On an anatomical level, never, ever forget how vulnerable a target those balls can be. Since a kick requires a lot more aim, go with a fist, open hand, elbow, or knee.

Repeat as needed.

Z (AS IN MICKEY)

Why do I feel qualified to write about self-defense for radicals?

- Well, first of all, I am a radical of sorts (or at least I aim to be every day).
- I'm probably the only person to appear in both a radical book with Noam Chomsky and a karate flick with Billy "Tae Bo" Blanks. In other words, I am a writer and a fighter.
- I've been fortunate enough to have many strong, loving women in my life—in particular my Mom and my wife/partner, Michele.
- And finally, who gives a shit about qualifications anyway? You don't need credentials to kick an oppressor's ass.

POSTSCRIPT

"Women who take self-defense instruction, with whatever motivation and ideological perspectives, are offered an implicit or explicit critique of the ways in which gender is constructed in a culture of male privilege which rests on the abuse of women. What is usually taken for granted as a fact of nature—that a woman simply cannot physically challenge a man—is revealed as a social script which privileges men at the expense of women. ... Self-defense offers the possibility of a critical consciousness of gender's influence on what we see as male and female bodies."

—MARTHA MCCAUGHEY, REAL KNOCKOUTS

BIOGRAPHY

The regular visitors to Mickey Z.'s website have ordained themselves "The Expendables." Mickey asked them to write a collective bio and here's the result:

Mickey Z.'s voice is the roundhouse kick of activist literature...profoundly mistrustful of government in all its dreadful guises, while courageously supporting all of us who stand against it. Determined to live the words, rather than simply to speak them, Mickey Z. doesn't get more readers, he just makes more friends. His blog is like a front stoop where we all gather to talk over the news, what's happening with each other, and generally enjoy each other's company. The gentle concern for his fellow humans and the behind-the-scenes acts of kindness are surpassed only by the cuteness of his dimples.

He can be found on the Web at: **WWW.MICKEYZ.NET**

ABOUT PM PRESS

PM Press was founded at the end of 2007 by a small collection of folks with decades of publishing, media, and organizing experience. We seek to create radical and stimulating fiction and non-fiction books, pamphlets, t-shirts, visual and audio materials to entertain, educate and inspire you. We aim to distribute these through every available channel with every available technology—whether that means you are seeing anarchist classics at our bookfair stalls; reading our latest vegan cookbook at the café; downloading geeky fiction e-books; or digging new music and timely videos from our website.

PM Press is always on the lookout for talented and skilled volunteers, artists, activists and writers to work with. If you have a great idea for a project or can contribute in some way, please get in touch.